PURSUE

21 Days of Prayer and Strategy at the Halftime of the Year

Bob Perry & Amy Joy Lykosh

MAKARIOS
PRESS

Esmont, VA

Makarios Press
P.O. Box 28, Esmont, VA 22937

Scripture in NIV unless otherwise stated.

Cover: Nate Braxton

ISBN 978-1-956561-24-1

Printed in the United States of America

CONTENTS

Pursue

1. *follow (someone or something) in order to catch them*

   ◦ seek to attain or accomplish (a goal) over a long period

2. *(of a person or way) continue or proceed along (a path or route)*

   ◦ engage in (an activity or course of action)
   ◦ continue to investigate, explore, or discuss (a topic, idea, or argument)

INTRODUCTION

An Invitation to Pursue: 21 Days of Prayer

But seek first his kingdom and his righteousness, and all these things will be given to you as well.[1]

I once met with a client who wanted to begin a major initiative, an unprecedented move forward. There was no roadmap to make it happen. And the client's initial proposal was: let's gather twice a week to pray for clarity on how to move forward.[2]

I thought: *This is so healing for me.*

For almost 40 years, I had been involved with the church world. I would go to planning meetings, and at the beginning I would ask, "Shouldn't we pray?"

And they would say, "Oh, Bob, yes! You are good at prayer! Please, open this meeting!"

And I would pray for two minutes, and then they would start to work on their agenda.

But here was someone in the business world who said, "We need more wisdom than we have. So let's spend some time in order to know from God how to move forward. As a group, let's seek God for wisdom."

With this story as a backdrop, I want to invite you to press in to prayer now, so that we can be ready to run well through the rest of this year.

If January is a time to detox and face forward, August is an excellent month to look to the harvest:

- Look with delight and gratitude at what the Lord has done already
- Honestly address the events of the year thus far
- Make any necessary course corrections
- Prepare to run the race with endurance

August is a month to break free of any shame, and seek God's face for the plan for the days to come.

And why the name "Pursue"?

It comes from the verse above, Matthew 6:33: "But seek first his kingdom and his righteousness, and all these things will be given to you as well."

How do you get all that you want in life?

Seek first his kingdom.

To "seek" means to attempt to find something, to ask for something from someone, to search for something.

Attempt to find God's kingdom. Ask for God's kingdom from God. Search for God's kingdom.

I once had the privilege to spend four days with Bill Johnson of Bethel Redding. He talks about how we seek first God's kingdom. Period. There is no second thing to seek.

Seek God's kingdom.

And one of the synonyms for "seek" is "pursue."

But, as with all synonyms, it's similar, but not identical, to "seek."

In the scripture, "pursue" is often a negative word, used of enemies in pursuit. This goes along with the definition "follow (someone or something) in order to catch them."

But, of course, "pursuit" is sometimes turned on its head.

Think of Psalm 23:6, that most famous of Psalms. "*So why would I fear the future?* Only goodness and tender love pursue me all the days of my life."[3]

Not all the things that pursue us are bad.

"Pursue" also has a sense of goals and accomplishments, of purpose and direction. The dictionary includes definitions like: seek to attain or accomplish a goal over a long period. Continue along a path. Engage in a course of action. Continue to investigate, explore, or discuss a topic, idea, or argument.[4]

This is a wonderful season to pursue the things of the Lord:

- Turn from evil and do good; seek peace and pursue it.[5]
- The LORD detests the way of the wicked, but he loves those who pursue righteousness.[6]
- But you, man of God, flee from all this, and pursue righteousness, godliness, faith, love, endurance and gentleness.[7]
- Flee the evil desires of youth and pursue righteousness, faith, love and peace, along with those who call on the Lord out of a pure heart.[8]

As we face the last few months of the year, we have dreams and goals and visions ... but we also get to pursue peace, righteousness, godliness, faith, love, endurance, gentleness.

Come on!

— Bob & Amy

TAKE INVENTORY

WHY AUGUST IS SO STRATEGIC

I'm a huge sports fan. To me, the August prayer intensive is like a halftime reset.

Sure, literally the year is more than half over. Mathematically, it's not actually the halfway point. At the start of August, we have lived through seven months of the year, and we have five months to go. But psychologically, August feels more like halfway than June.

One school semester has passed, and we have one to go. Depending on the year and the holidays, we have about 100 normal working days left in the year.

We're at the halftime break, and coming in to the second real push of the year.

In sports, it used to be that what took place in the first half and what took place in the second half didn't change that much. Maybe a good coach would come up with some new plays at halftime, drawing their ideas on a blackboard.

That's no longer the case.

Today the good coaches have a different game plan for the first half of the game and the second. They treat one game as two separate games, with different plays for each half. The great teams are feared coming out of halftime because they have a creative game plan for the second half.

This is why you can find tremendous swings from one

quarter to the next.

But this volatility is also true for businesses. One of our clients had one of the best first quarters of his company's history, but then the second quarter was the worst quarter of the company's history. Volatility.

For another client, their former bread-and-butter product, high-end fireplaces, started to decline, but their new line of outdoor furniture is breaking every record. The rebalancing of product lines kept them in the black. But still: volatility.

With all of this change, we invite you to spend 21 days to pause and prepare to take a bit of time to pause and prepare for the second half of the year.

Recognize that the Lord can catch up any loss that you've had in the first seven months. It's not too late to turn things around. If you've been knocked out, or if you're numb, or if you're in survival mode, you can reignite your dream again.

And if things are going well? If you've got the momentum, you've got the hot hand? Lean in! More prayer simply increases the momentum and allows you to make any adjustments you need to.

During my time in the corporate world, we would occasionally take a look at our sales goals. Were we on track? What did we need to shift for the months to come? We had made goals and had aspirations at the beginning of the year. How was our progress toward those goals?

Most people lagged behind. This time for reflection became a reality check.

Those who took a midyear pause enjoyed a competitive advantage over those who didn't.

It is also possible—because we live in the real world—that you find that your target has changed. Maybe the Lord will say, "The plan that looked good in January fit in that season, but now we have a different target. Don't go on automatic pilot, pursuing the same vision without checking in."

Seven months into the year, we can examine: is the Lord

shifting us? What we thought the Lord was asking us to do at the start of the year—is that still his invitation? Or have we mostly accomplished it, and he's inviting us to the next thing?

Whether we need to double down on our original goals, or adjust our goals altogether, either way, we need to seed the ground with prayer.

And what better time to do this than a time when your schedule is still in flux?

In August, most people aren't in their standard rhythm yet, not yet in their daily routine. Most of us are trying to recover from summer. We're thinking of school starting, or vacation ending. We might be a bit disconnected from work and relationships, a bit scattered, a bit unfocused.

Over the years, I would fast in the summer. Ten days here, twenty-one days there, maybe in June, maybe in July, maybe in August.

The Lord always met me, and it was always beautiful, but it had no rhyme or reason.

So it fascinated me when Chris Hodges, of Church of the Highlands in Birmingham, started a 21-day time of intensive prayer ... in August.

Chris called his staff together and said, "Let's regroup with 21 days of focused prayer for our community. People can fast if they have a desire, but we need to focus and realign. What have we done so far this year? What is our vision for the rest of the year?"

Then they would pray into their goals, their desires.

In the church community, they made their list of who they were praying would come to know Christ, or who was struggling in their faith. They would pray for their dream for the women's ministry, or the children's ministry.

Then, from this place of prayerful intentionality, in September, when programs started up again, they were already covered in prayer.

They prayed in advance for the work yet to come. They had

an intentional sowing into their fall ministry and outreach.

But this concept isn't just for the church world.

In the book of Nehemiah, when Nehemiah heard that the walls of Jerusalem were still broken down, he prayed for four months. Then he suddenly got all of the supplies he needed, and when he reached Jerusalem, it took him and the residents less than two months to rebuild the walls.[9]

He sowed in prayer in order to reap a harvest of production and protection.

This is the invitation to us in August: pray in advance of what we want to see the rest of this year. Invite God into the picture.

Instead of just willpower, or gritting our teeth through the practical aspects of leadership training and goal setting, hard work and diligence, here we invite God to help us.

We invite God to speak, to inform, to redirect.

God has a blueprint for our lives. Are we building according to his blueprint?

Listen and hear what God is speaking.

PRAY BECAUSE PRAYER WORKS

One of my foundational principles is that *prayer works.* The first day I met Amy in person, she remembers me saying, "If prayer didn't work, why would we bother? We need to see results!"

Think about the Lord's Prayer.

It's so simple that anyone could pray it, including the original, uneducated followers of Jesus.

Our Father, which art in heaven, hallowed be thy name.

This prayer begins with a beautiful praise.

Thy kingdom come, thy will be done on earth, as it is in heaven.

This is results-based. "Bring the stability of heaven to the shakiness of this earth."

And we expect that to happen because we've asked for it.

Give us this day our daily bread.

We expect that provision, because if we didn't, why would we bother? We need that provision, day by day.

Forgive us our debts, as we forgive our debtors.

Keep us in right relationship with other people.

This is so practical for business! Every business person runs into situations—disagreements with coworkers, problems with vendors, etc.

We all become debtors. We all need to be forgiven.

We all become creditors. We all need to forgive.

And lead us not into temptation, but deliver us from evil.
We need to actually have that protection.
For thine is the kingdom and the power and the glory forever. Amen.[10]

Amen and amen!

Notice how much of this prayer expects outcomes!

And, in truth, Jesus himself wanted results.

Hebrews 12:2 says of Jesus, "For the joy set before him he endured the cross, scorning its shame, and sat down at the right hand of the throne of God."

Jesus had a reward promised: the joy set before him. He was expecting an outcome. A payment, if you will.

Never give in to the idea that God isn't transactional!

Jesus knew what the reward would be, and he pursued it.

The record of the scripture is that Jesus cared about results. He also cared about business, he cared about righteous business owners, and he cared about prayer.

May God's kingdom expand!

NO, REALLY...
PRAYER WORKS

A church in North America decided to test the efficacy of prayer. This church took a neighborhood of 160 houses and split it into two sections of 80 houses each. The church asked the congregation to pray for one section of 80 houses.

Mission India founder John DeVries wrote about what happened next.

———— • ✺ • ————

After the set period of prayer, the church secretary contacted all 160 homes, asking the same question and using the same approach. By phone she told them who she was, explained that the church was willing to include all who lived in the neighborhood in their prayer program, and asked if they had any specific prayer requests for which the church could intercede. She also offered to have a couple call if the neighbors had matters they would like to talk about for prayer. When she called the 80 homes that had not been prayed for, she found that only one person responded with a prayer request. But when she called the 80 homes that have been deliberately prayed for, she found to her amazement that 67 of these families responded with prayer requests, and more than 40 of them asked for visits from the church!

This is what Jesus had in mind when he spoke about "rest."

When we are yoked to Jesus and we begin on the foot he
begins with—that is, prayer—our task is lifted up in the wind
of the Spirit and supernaturally sails along.

I learned this lesson in a unique way in my work for Mission
India. While attending a prayer seminar, I was challenged to
choose, if I were a pastor, between hiring a full-time director
of music or a full-time "pray-er" for the church. It took me
only a moment to decide that I wanted the "professional"
intercessor. I got so excited about the idea that I challenged
the board of Mission India to change the job description of
one of our staff members to be exactly that....

I shared this story with a friend in India, who then told
me that God led him to do much the same thing in the same
year—1992. He had labored with his little mission in a city
in the heart of India for about ten years, and fewer than
twenty little house churches had started. He and his wife were
burned out and tired. He then decided to hire "professional"
intercessors and to begin his mission work in prayer, not
with human effort. A few years later, he had twenty-two
people reporting for prayer work every day! And the mission
exploded to more than 160 little house churches in those
few years.

Are you being "carried" along by Jesus on the wind of the
Holy Spirit, or are you trying to carry Jesus along? It may be
so simple a model as being out of step with the Savior. To be
yoked is to be *in step*—and when that happens, we find that the
task is easy and light, for He is pulling with us. When prayer
is first and work is second, we are in step with Jesus. With the
work arising out of prayer, we shift from working in human
power to working in divine power.[11]

PRAYER WORKS EVEN MORE POWERFULLY WHEN WE ADD FASTING

During this 21 days of prayer, the focus is less on fasting and self-sacrifice, and more about pressing in to hear the Lord's voice.

If you feel no desire to fast, that's no problem.

But maybe you're curious about fasting.

With fasting, we give up a little bit, and then the Lord gives us incredible gifts.

With all the amazing variations of possible fasts, I appreciated this simple idea: four main categories of fasting.

Most of the options below don't require calorie restriction. With most of these options, you can eat enough to avoid hunger pangs. Some of the options are safe for pregnant and nursing women.

1. A Complete Fast.

With this option, people drink only liquids. Some do only water. Others add fresh pressed juices, bone broth.

This is generally not the place to start. To be safe, this type of fast requires fairly intense attention to your health and well-being.

2. A Selective Fast

You might think of this like a Lenten fast.

Many people give up something during Lent.

You might give up one thing (sugar, chocolate, wine).

Or you might give up a category of things (all beverages other than water—or water and coffee, if necessary).

Or you might choose a specific set of ingredients to focus on.

A Daniel Fast, for example, would be a version of this, where a person eats foods sown or grown. A vegan diet.

Or only whole, unprocessed foods, like the Whole30.

Another example would be a liquid-only diet. With this, you could do smoothies, soups, protein drinks. Apparently Irish monks developed Guinness so they wouldn't be hungry during fast days. Nothing like drinking 1,000 calories in each stein to keep the hunger pangs at bay.

Amy did this once for a week, and though she wasn't hungry, she was surprised by how much she missed the sensation of chewing.

3. A Partial Fast

Also called an intermittent fast, or a Jewish fast.

With this fast, you opt to only eat during certain hours of the day.

For example, "I will eat for eight hours and not eat for sixteen hours."

So with this, you'd stop eating at, say, 8pm, then you would eat again at noon the next day.

If you are used to grazing during most of your waking hours, it could be that you start with 12 hours on and 12 hours off, and every few days adjust the window by a half hour.

Fascinating sidenote: cutting-edge doctors promote intermittent fasting as one of the best options you can do for your health. It allows your body a chance to turn focus away from digestion and to clean up.

For my wife Sharon, when no other weight loss program worked, intermittent fasting was the magic bullet.

So is a partial fast simply a chance to walk in the health that's our birthright?

It's something to think about.

4. A Soul Fast

If you aren't in a place to give up food of any type ... that's fine! If you're pregnant, or nursing, or deal with low blood sugar, or have a history of eating disorders, or for some other reason that makes a food restriction a challenge ... that's no problem! You can do something to support your soul.

If you think about it, God established the Sabbath, so that one day in seven we would rest from our work.

I think that counts as an example of a soul fast.

Other examples: you might step away from a particular social media that has gotten a bit out of control, or stop critical self-talk, or believing that the scriptures don't apply to you.

You might decide to focus well on forgiving. As often as angry thoughts arise, you consciously forgive.

You might do a negativity fast, where you turn away from negative self-talk.

Basically, a soul fast is any way that you feel the Lord is calling you to turn away from something and renew your mind towards a new thought pattern.

How to Choose

With a 21-day fast, you don't have to do the same thing the whole time. Feel free to pick and choose, if more than one option calls to you.

Some possibilities:

- You could do a fast for the five workdays and skip the weekends.
- You could do different options during different days or weeks: a Daniel fast five days of the week, and a complete fast on Tuesday and Friday.
- You could do a calorie reduction the first week, then liquid only the second week, then a complete fast for the third week, and then transition back to life after that.
- You could do a half week of reduced calories, a half week of liquid only, a week of complete fast, and then reverse back: a half week of liquid only, and a half week of reduced calories, and then you are back to normal.

So many different possibilities. Listen to the Lord and ask him what he would have you do for these three weeks.

And if the answer is, "Just pray," then "just pray" with thanksgiving.

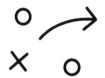

FIRST HALF REVIEW

Day 1: Morning
GOODNESS AND LOVINGKINDNESS PURSUE YOU

Tracking you down

In Psalm 23, David says "Surely goodness and lovingkindness will follow me all the days of my life."[12]

Goodness and lovingkindness are not following like a puppy following a master.

No. Wrong.

A better translation would be, "Goodness and lovingkindness are tracking me down."

The word "follow" means, "to run after (usually with hostile intent), chase, put to flight, follow, hunt, pursue."[13]

David, the shepherd and the man of war, flips this violent word on its head. Instead of enemies pursuing, now God's goodness and lovingkindness pursue.

They're pursuing you.

In our lives, we live in this virtuous circle of pursuit, where God pursues us, and we pursue God.

Paul Van Hoesen prayed this gorgeous blessing out of Psalm 23:6.

———————— • ✳ • ————————

"Surely goodness and lovingkindness will follow me all the days of my life, and I will dwell in the house of the Lord forever."

I declare that over you today, that goodness and lovingkindness are stalking you right now.

They're following you around.

You don't see them. They're behind you. They're in front of you. They're next to you.

The Lord's goodness and lovingkindness are looking out for you when you're not even aware, listening to every heartbeat, every thought, every desire.

The Lord is following you today with goodness and lovingkindness, and his goodness and lovingkindness are following you around, waiting to spring to life when you least expect it.

And the great promise we have: we will dwell in the house of the Lord forever.

Father, I ask you to release today an awareness of eternity.

I do a lot of deals, and the greatest investment we can make is to invest in eternity.

So we thank you, Father, for the amazing promises today, that we will dwell in your house forever.

I release that awareness over us today.

Goodness and lovingkindness will follow us, and we will know that we are in God's hands forever.

In Jesus' name, amen.

Day 1: Evening
PURSUE COMFORT

A basic request that's easy to overlook

I once spent a week in Malibu at a retreat called The Father's Heart. Several speakers talked about a prayer that I had never thought of before—even after 40 years of asking for the Lord to teach me to pray! There's always more to learn!

Here's the prayer:

Comfort me, Father.
Comfort me, Jesus.
Comfort me, Holy Spirit.
Comfort me.

This is such a basic request!

And yet, even though I know from the scriptures that the Holy Spirit is called the Comforter, or the Advocate,[14] I don't necessarily think of God as someone who would be delighted to give me comfort.

As you pray, as you listen, as you consider, I encourage you to ask:

Comfort me, Father.
Comfort me, Jesus.
Comfort me, Holy Spirit.
Comfort me.

Another perspective on the Holy Spirit as the "Comforter": a warm quilt is sometimes called a "comforter." *The Passion Translation* refers repeatedly to God's "wraparound presence." Want comfort, like a warm hug, a warm quilt? Here are some scriptures to enjoy.

- God, your wraparound presence is my shield. You bring victory to all who are pure in heart.[15]
- Because I set you, Yahweh, always close to me, my confidence will never be weakened, for I experience your wraparound presence every moment.[16]
- I stand silently to listen for the one I love, waiting as long as it takes for the Lord to rescue me. For God alone has become my Savior. He alone is my safe place; his wraparound presence always protects me. For he is my champion defender; there's no risk of failure with God. So why would I let worry paralyze me, even when troubles multiply around me?[17]
- God, your wraparound presence is our defense. In your kindness look upon the faces of your anointed ones.[18]

Day 2: Morning
PURSUE THE PRIZE

Because every day is a good day to run

Therefore, since we are surrounded by such a great cloud of witnesses, let us throw off everything that hinders and the sin that so easily entangles. And let us run with perseverance the race marked out for us, fixing our eyes on Jesus, the pioneer and perfecter of faith. For the joy set before him he endured the cross, scorning its shame, and sat down at the right hand of the throne of God.[19]

Look back at how far you have run already this year, how much you've accomplished.

Then prayerfully consider *how* you have run.

Do you not know that in a race all the runners run, but only one gets the prize? Run in such a way as to get the prize. Everyone who competes in the games goes into strict training. They do it to get a crown that will not last; but we do it to get a crown that will last forever.[20]

If overall I ran hard and well, but I can also look back and say, "Oh, I remember that week. Oof. That was a week where I wanted to go into hiding. And, yes, I remember that month. I was not as focused as I could be."

How do I—how do *we*—deal with those places of missing

the mark?

We can always pray!

———— ·✲· ————

Lord Jesus, thank you for your graciousness. Thank you for the metaphors of life, such as a runner, running the race. Lord, thank you for your gentleness to us, to guide and direct us, and that if we start to get a little bit off course, that you send corrections to us.

Lord, for any of the ways that, over the last seven months, we have gotten off course, we ask, Lord, that you would forgive us and wipe us clean, remove the extra weights.

For any places where we took our eyes from the prize, where, instead of being focused we were distracted, Lord, thank you that you always have a solution.

In this case, the solution looks like confessing to you the short-coming, turning back to you, and again fixing our eyes on the prize as we run with patience and endurance.

Give us clarity and grace to do that in for the rest of this year. May we finish this course well.

Thank you, Jesus.

Amen.

Day 2: Evening
PURSUE FELLOWSHIP

Because sometimes we need a rebalancing

The Godhead demonstrates how God relates within himself: living in perfect communion, perfect harmony and love.

As we go through life, most of us experience occasional shaking in our relationships, a rebalancing of how we spend our time, and with whom.

You might ask the Lord a few questions as you go about your day.

Do I have any relationships that need to be strengthened?

Perhaps you realize that you're not paying as much attention to spouse or children as you would prefer. Perhaps the Lord reminds you of a friend that you love that you could reach out to in the next few months.

Do I have any relationships that need to be jettisoned?

Perhaps a certain colleague needs to be avoided. Perhaps a Bible study companion is less good for you than you expected.

Do I have any relationships that need to be repaired?

Perhaps you need to ask for forgiveness.

Perhaps you need to extend forgiveness.

In either case, after forgiveness, you might wish to retain the relationship, or you might wish to end it.

The offer of forgiveness is one of the most critical things we can do for our own mental health, and for our physical health as well.

———— •❀• ————

Why Forgiveness Requires More Than an "I'm Sorry"

In Amy's family of origin, they differentiated between "I'm sorry" and "please forgive me."

"I'm sorry" meant, "I wish that had not happened. Bummer."

It implied no real wrong-doing, more like a regret over a missed opportunity.

"Please forgive me" was much deeper.

It assumed culpability and responsibility.

It assumed wrong-doing, and the need for repentance in order to restore the relationship.

Forgiveness requires several steps.

Amy shares an example of a conversation she once had with a new acquaintance, where she felt judged for her appearance, her intellect, and her walk with God.

Painful.

She might never speak to this person again.

So how could she move forward, when maybe that one didn't even intend to cause pain?

Here was her recovery process.

1. Acknowledge the whole hurt.

Lord, this person judged me. This person hurt me. This person assumed certain things about me.
Speak the whole truth to the Lord, as you see it.

2. Extend forgiveness.

Lord, I know you say, "But if you do not forgive others their sins, your Father will not forgive your sins."[21] *I need your forgiveness, Lord, and I do not want any corrosive presence in my life. So I choose to forgive this person.*
Quick caveat here: this prayer does not mean that you need an ongoing relationship. It simply means that you are not holding anything against them.

3. Receive healing.

This step is easy to miss.
Healing and restoration most likely looks slightly different, depending on the offense. But in this example, Amy prayed:
Lord, I don't want any connection with this person. I take the sword of the Spirit, dipped in the blood of Jesus, and I cut myself free from any inappropriate tie that I might have with that one.
I ask, Lord, that you bring back to me any pieces of myself that one took. And I take the Holy Spirit magnet over my body to remove any barbs, nails, or metal bits that were stuck in me, and I hand all those metal bits to you, Jesus, as I don't want them.
I pour the Holy Spirit oil, the balm of Gilead, over all the hurt places, the bruised places, and ask for healing and restoration for all places that still need to be made whole. Thank you, Lord.

4. Extend blessing.

For an unbeliever, the greatest blessing would be repentance and conversion, and that's a beautiful thing to ask on someone

else's behalf. *Bless this one, your creation, with you, Lord.*
But for a brother or sister in Christ, bless them.

Lord, I ask that you bless this one. Bless their family, bless their ministry, bless the work of their hands. May they prosper in the ways of the Lord.

Thank you, Lord, for your graciousness, your forgiveness, your restoration, and your blessing.

Thank you that I get to be part of your plan for redeeming the world.

In the precious name of Jesus, amen.

Day 3: Morning
PURSUE LEVITY

Because God is a God of delight

Amy's first introduction to me came via a recording. My friend Paul Van Hoesen and I spoke at a Heaven in Business conference about how to pray for businesses.

She said later, "If I had to pick one word to describe Bob at that season of his life, it would be *earnest*.

"He delivered his message with a bit of the flavor of the Old Testament prophet. A focused, serious, intense presentation.

"After all, prayer for businesses *matters*, and he wanted to make sure the audience understood what he was trying to communicate."

As an excellent student, Amy acknowledged the beauty of that focus, diligence, and zeal. We don't want to take our responsibilities lightly.

On the other hand, she thought: *I don't picture Jesus scowling at his disciples when he went to teach them. Rather, I think he spoke from a heart of compassion and love, still focused and committed to the Father's business, but with more of an aspect of good humor and kindness, rather than grave solemnity.*

A few years later, she doesn't think of me as "earnest" any more.

Passionate, committed, diligent: yes.

But I am seeking to inhabit a space that is more delight-driven, more playful. Less humorless, sober, hard-working, grave.

Still thoughtful, still dedicated. But enjoying life.

And so, as we go through these days of listening to the Father, listening to the Son, listening to the Holy Spirit, my encouragement to you is to celebrate the God who made the porcupine, the platypus, and the pineapple, who sends cardinals with their flash of red amidst the green foliage, the God who put the amazing ability to change and adjust into the genetic code, and who expresses unique facets of himself in more than seven billion different ways.

This loving, playful God delights in you, his child, and invites you to come and fellowship with him.

———— • ✳ • ————

Lord, may we enjoy the journey with you. Amen!

Day 3: Evening
PURSUE YOUR GIFTING

Because that's your point of greatest impact

Once I went on a retreat where person after person prayed over me that I would have the ability to play, to enjoy life.

This was so unexpected, I asked Sharon if she was getting those same prayers. I wondered if maybe this was simply the theme of the prayer warriors that week.

No.

These prayers were specific to me.

For almost 12 years, I served as a missionary to Latvia, during the time when it came out from under Communist rule. After decades of difficult living as part of the Soviet Union, the people had so little joy. It had been wrung out of them.

I would walk the streets, with my considerable energy and bouncing step, and think, "This is so odd, that the Lord would send me, an enthusiastic American, to this nation of people who are mostly pretty dour. It's a real cultural mismatch."

So why did people pray over *me*, an enthusiastic and energetic person, that I would *play*?

Well, first, *enthusiasm* is not the same as *play*. They may overlap, but they are not identical. I might be enthusiastic, but that doesn't imply that I am also playful.

But I also took this away: even the things that we think we know well, we find more layers and more levels.

How do we make the biggest impact?

Not by shoring up our weaknesses, but by maximizing our strengths.

For my co-author Amy, it makes more sense for her to focus on improving her writing and improving in prayer than it does for her to try to develop coding skills. She doesn't like coding, and we can hire that out.

For me, for years I used to try to write books. But then every time I would start, I would think, *My point of greatest impact is going to be in intercession.*

And so I would go and pray. But I also asked the Lord to make me a good story-teller, a good speaker.

And now Amy and I work together, using our different skills.

And now we get to add more playfulness.

How might this apply to you?

So often in a community, what the leader carries then reproduces in the lives of that community.

We want to bless you with the knowledge of your highest and best use, and, as you work in your strengths, with the ability to be light and playful.

———— • ✦ • ————

Lord, as we have had gifts imparted to us, we impart now to these, our brothers and sisters, that they would have an uptick in their ability to understand their unique gifts and callings, and that they would operate out of the lightness and playfulness that you offer.

Thank you, Jesus. In your precious name. Amen.

Day 4: Morning
PURSUE REMEMBRANCE

Because we all have problems we need to overcome

A little past the midpoint of the year, spend some of your moments today remembering what God has done for you.

Seven months is both an enormous amount of time, and, usually, a small fraction of a life.

Bill Johnson taught an outstanding message on remembering the deeds of the Lord, out of one of his favorite passages, Mark 8.

The disciples were talking about how they had forgotten bread. Jesus asked them, "Why do you reason because you have no bread? Do you not yet perceive nor understand? Is your heart still hardened? Having eyes, do you not see? And having ears, do you not hear? And do you not remember?"[22]

Jesus doesn't ever correct to shame or mock, but rather corrects so that the listener could change. He invites the hearer to repent from a hard heart.

Jesus asked his disciples several questions, but let's look at these three:

1. *Having eyes, do you not see?*
2. *And having ears, do you not hear?*

3. And do you not remember?

Bill Johnson pointed out that we might think of the first two senses, the first two questions, as unique and extraordinary gifts.
Oh, that person is so perceptive—but maybe I'm not.
Oh, that person hears so clearly—but maybe I don't.
But memory?
Memory, remembering, is a product of our will.
We don't think of memory as a gift. It's a decision, a focus, an intention.
I can always remember. Become selective on what you recall and think about. Jesus wants their history with God to be the lenses through which they see the present problem."[23]
When Jesus fed the multitude, those who ate the bread had their immediate needs satisfied. That was great.
But at the heart, the point of the miracle was not to entertain. Jesus didn't want the disciples to remember the miracle to make the disciples happy about a past event.
No. The call to the disciples was far greater: they must change how they think and see, lest the miracle fail to have its full effect.
The disciples needed to learn to see from another place, so they wouldn't be intimidated by a problem.
To do that, they needed to *remember.*

———— • ❀ • ————

Lord Jesus, you asked the disciples, "And do you not remember?"
I confess, Lord, that I do not do a good job remembering. You have proven yourself faithful to me again and again. I want to renew my mind, so let me rehearse your goodness, let me dwell on your grace, let me focus on what you are doing in this world. Thank you. Amen.

Day 4: Evening
PURSUE ENDURING STRENGTH

Because we want to be effective for 70 or 80 years

Dear friend, I pray that you may enjoy good health and that all may go well with you, even as your soul is getting along well.[24]

When I was a young man, I had a season where I chauffeured spiritual giants to and from the airport, men like Loren Cunningham, the founder of YWAM. These were men in their early 60s, faithful and beautiful.

All of them had dealt with the early loss of a friend because these friends hadn't cared for their bodies.

It shook me, to realize that we could literally face the loss of years, or even decades, because of the food and lifestyle choices we make when we're young.

As you reflect on the last seven months, think about how you physically managed your body, what Paul calls "the temple of the Holy Spirit."[25]

Do you need to add anything, like more exercise or strength and conditioning?

Do you need to make any adjustments to your diet?

Are you taking any medications that you potentially could

quit with some form of lifestyle change?

None of these questions come from a place of condemnation. What's done is done.

Rather, simply evaluate overall.

In Psalm 90, Moses (who lived to be 120) wrote, "Our days may come to seventy years, or eighty, if our strength endures."[26]

A decade or two ago, Amy was horrified to read about how often women in their 60s get to the point where they can no longer lift their grocery bags, because they have not done physical labor enough to maintain their strength.

She said, "I don't particularly like doing push-ups ... but that might be something I need to add."

Wherever you are in your health journey, bring your life before the Lord.

———— · ✳ · ————

Lord, highlight any place where I could be doing better, and then let me do better. May I do all I can to be in peak physical and mental condition for as many of my days as possible.

Day 5: Morning
PURSUE A WAY FORWARD

With freedom and joy

Going through a box of unread books, Amy came across one called *God, Improv, and the Art of Living*.

A friend of hers once said, "When I cared for my mother with dementia, I realized I needed to live with the idea of improv. She would say something entirely random, and, as the caretaker, I wouldn't say, "Well, that's ridiculous!" and try to correct her, but rather say, "Oh, yes. And tell me more!"

Such a creative perspective!

People who do improv always say yes!

"A mentor liked to remind her seminary classes that the book of Exodus—the story of God's liberation of the people of Israel from slavery into the Promised Land—has a clue about the nature of God right in the title. 'Exodus' is a Greek word and literally means 'a way out.'

"Not *the* way out, *a* way out. This subtle commentary says something of the infinite creativity of God. This doesn't sound like a God who planned how everything was going to turn out down to the last detail. This is a God who worked with the situation at hand. The 'how' of God's work is incidental; the overarching Yes of liberation is God's fundamental focus."[27]

Now, theologically, this is getting into deep waters of predestination and free will.

But what a beautiful picture of God saying, "I am offering you a way out. Will you take it?"

And when the children of Israel do, they soon come to a place with the Red Sea before, and an army of enemies behind.

Don't worry—there is, again, a way out.

At every step, Moses does the next thing.

And God always has a solution.

———— •❈• ————

We ask the Lord to bless you this day with the ability to approach problems from a spirit of improvisation, with the knowledge that whatever it is that you are working on, that God has a solution, and that you get to move forward with the information that you have, and because of the astonishing greatness of God, what you have is enough.

Day 5: Evening
PURSUE FREEDOM TO MOVE FORWARD

Because the Lord is always up to something

Amy told me about the astonishing idea that the title of the book of Exodus means, "A way out."

What freedom! We can simply choose what to do next!

I prayed, "Lord, the accuser says, 'You should have been in this line in the grocery store, because it would have gone faster. You should have taken this route, and then gone that way. You should have said this or that. You should have invested here or there. You should have taken your money there and gotten a quicker return.'

"Now, Lord, I could feel this breaking free. I could feel this unkind voice silenced, and Lord, this setting free, where we get to do improv. It's part of a dance. It's part of growing it's part of maturity. It's part of the journey. We welcome a good, good Father."

Amy then told me this story.

———— • ✳ • ————

Recently I went to the grocery store with a friend. We only had a few items to check out. Of the two open checkout lines, one seemed to be pretty much finished, so we headed there.

And we stood there.

And we stood there.

And we stood there.

Sometimes, apparently, the first three payment methods don't work.

And, sure, we could have swept up the seven items from the conveyor belt and moved over to the other lane. But that sense that, "Surely she's just about done" prevailed.

Conversation in a checkout line is a bit awkward, because you know that whatever you're talking about is going to be interrupted at any moment, and then you'll pivot to make small talk with the cashier.

I grew a bit agitated. *This is precious time with my friend, and I'm wasting it! We picked the wrong line!*

But what a revelation to me!

What if, when I go to the grocery store next, I don't assume that the winning strategy is to pick the fastest lane and get out as quickly as possible?

What if, instead, I listen to the voice of the Holy Spirit and watch for what he's doing? What if I ask which lane I should go to, and, once there, say, "Why am I here? Am I supposed to pray for the people around me? Am I supposed to listen in silence to you? Do I engage with the person next to me and ask if I can pray for them? Do I pay attention and see if I can sense some agitation in the environment, and speak peace over those who are frustrated?"

If my entire framework for decision-making has been about one outcome—getting out of the grocery store the fastest—I've shut off a lot of other possible avenues where the Lord might be working.

————— • ✸ • —————

Lord, as we extrapolate this out to our lives—how exciting! We stand astonished at the additional ways that you want to speak into our days!

Lord, when we think of all of the different ways that, over the course of a lifetime, we can look back and feel like we really messed up ... thank you that you are always with us, always able to work good in a situation.

Thank you that you don't measure our lives in terms of wins and losses, but that you invite us instead to co-labor with you, learning to hear your voice.

Lord, teach us your ways. May we be attentive. Thank you, Lord. Amen.

Day 6: Morning
PURSUE CELEBRATION

Because none of us get enough cheers

Marketing expert Perry Marshall once talked about how, as an entrepreneur, we can get in this pattern of doing things that no one else does, and then, after accomplishing them, we immediately turn to the next thing.

But, in truth, God is a God of celebration.

Take Deuteronomy 14:22-28.

The children of Israel were to take ten percent of their gross yield and turn it into a celebration.

Not profit! Gross!

This tithe is not the same as the standard Old Testament "ten percent to support the Levites" tithe.

Rather, this ten percent was specifically designated for a massive blow-out celebration, a feast to honor God, intended not only for the Israelites themselves, but also for the Levites, the foreigners, the orphans, and the widows.

Turning now to the New Testament, we come to the surprising scene where Jesus turns the water into wine for a wedding celebration where the guests had already had too much to drink.[28]

Not that drunkenness is an ideal celebration, but I love

that sense that Jesus was, apparently, far less uptight than we might imagine, far more willing to enter in to celebration.

So spend some time thinking back over the things worth celebrating this year. What went well? What can you celebrate?

Did you have any projects with progress or completion?

Did the Lord give you new ideas to run with?

It's not vanity to celebrate!

It's actually humility, to acknowledge how the Lord has been at work.

———— · ✸ · ————

Lord God, I don't know if the Israelites ever practiced the crazy party tithe, but I thank you for the picture of lavish celebration, simply because you're that good.

Thank you that, yes, you like work, and, yes, you like worship, but thank you that you also like celebration!

Thank you, Jesus, that you, too, celebrated. Thank you that you included your community in the celebration.

Teach us to celebrate with you, and to rejoice over the good things you have done in our lives.

You are so very good.

Thank you, Jesus. Amen.

Day 6: Evening
PURSUE OBEDIENT THOUGHTS

Because God likes even the numbers 6 and 13

Amy and I were talking on a Friday the Thirteenth about how easy it is for us to separate things into "good" and "bad."

The number five, the number of grace? Good!

The number seven, the number of perfection and completion? Good!

The number six? As in today, the sixth day of prayer? Oooh. Not so good.

And the number thirteen?

Worse and worse!

But let's press back against that idea.

Because thirteen? If someone asked Mary and Martha, "How many people are coming for dinner," the answer would have been: thirteen. Jesus and the disciples.

Has the enemy taken a beautiful number and distorted it for evil?

Or what about six?

Yes, sure, it's one short of perfection, and so might signify imperfection, the number of man.

But on the sixth day, the Lord finished creation.

Day One: light and dark, which corresponds to Day Four: the decorations: sun, moon, and stars.

Day Two: waters above and waters beneath, which corresponds to Day Five: the decorations: birds and fish.

Day Three: dry land, which corresponds to Day Six: the decorations: all plants, animals.

And man.

"You have made them a little lower than the angels and crowned them with glory and honor."[29]

This is a day set apart for the Lord.

As is every day.

———————— • ✴ • ————————

Lord, as we walk the land, may we remember that this is your territory, that we get to walk this place that you created and that you love, and that you are making all things new.

Lord, I think about how theologian Abraham Kuyper, back in 1880, said, "There is not a square inch in the whole domain of our human existence over which Christ, who is Sovereign over all, does not cry, Mine!"

How awesome a statement, Lord!

And you cry that not only over every square inch, but over every number, including six and thirteen. You cry that over every thought, because you tell us to take them captive. You cry that over every bit of our lives.

We want you to have it all, Lord. We are yours.

Lord, as Paul wrote, "We demolish arguments and every pretension that sets itself up against the knowledge of God, and we take captive every thought to make it obedient to Christ,"[30] we want our thoughts to align with yours. We want captive thoughts that obey you.

In the name of Jesus, amen.

Day 7: Morning
PURSUE POTENTIAL

Because God specializes in order out of chaos

Now the earth was formless and empty, darkness was over the surface of the deep, and the Spirit of God was hovering over the waters.[31]

Do you think this verse means something like: "the Spirit hovered over chaos and darkness"?

Perhaps.

But one book offered an interesting change of perspective.

"[C]haos does not mean disorder or confusion. Rather, it is a void, pregnant with possibility, from which creation can now occur. This is the concept of chaos that is given to us in the first chapter of Genesis. The Greeks referred to chaos as a state of becoming, not a state of disarray Science refers to chaos as a colloidal state out of which structure can be created. The entire physical universe was created out of chaos, and our physical bodies are created out of the product of our digestion—which is chaos, unorganized but fecund."[32]

When the Spirit broods over the darkness, instead consider that "the Spirit hovered [brooded, incubated] over infinite possibility."

So if you find yourself in a swirl, think, "This is simply unrealized potential. What will God make of it?"

———— • ✹ • ————

Lord, be at work in us! In our order and our potential! Amen!

Day 7: Evening
PURSUE WHAT'S COMING NEXT

And pray about what that is

As we come to the end of Week One, we pivot from what has passed and turn to what is to come.

For the next two weeks, we'll explore, in a variety of different ways, what the Lord is speaking to us about his plans for the months to come.

———·❋·———

Lord Jesus, thank you for the beautiful New English Translation of Isaiah 11:2: "The Lord's Spirit will rest on him—a Spirit that gives extraordinary wisdom, a Spirit that provides the ability to execute plans, a Spirit that produces absolute loyalty to the Lord."

This is what we cry out for, Lord. We need your wisdom as we face forward toward all that you have for us.

Blow out the cobwebs and the distractions. Give us clarity and direction.

In the name of Jesus, amen.

THE GAME
PLAN

Day 8: Morning
PURSUE THE EXPECTATION OF GOOD

And the breakthroughs that come, too

Paul Van Hoesen was giving a talk at a Heaven in Business conference. He said, "There is always a solution."

When Amy first heard that, she thought, "Wow. If that was true, that would really change everything."

Some months later, I sent her a list of Bill Johnson quotes.

She read through, and one of lines said: "The disciples were not accustomed to having breakthroughs."

"YES," she thought. "That matches my experience."

So she was chagrined when she returned to that quote and realized she had misread one of the words, and that it was actually a double negative.

Bill Johnson had actually said, "The disciples were not accustomed to *not* having breakthroughs."

Meaning: they *were* accustomed to *having* breakthroughs.

The disciples expected breakthroughs as their normal life.

For months she coming back to these two thoughts.

1. *There is always a solution.*
2. *The disciples were not accustomed to not having breakthroughs.*

She wondered: *do I live as if those statements are true? Or, despite God's creativity in creation, and Jesus' defeat of the enemy by his death and resurrection, do I expect roadblocks and defeat?*

There's a song with a line that keeps ringing in my head: "Whose report will we believe? We shall believe the report of the Lord!"

———— •✳• ————

"Let Your lovingkindness, O LORD, be upon us, according as we have hoped in You."[33]

Teach us what it means to expect your good, and receive a proportionate amount of lovingkindness.

Except, in truth, your lovingkindness is beyond imagining.

We ask that you would bless us with a greater expectation of good. We want to experience your lovingkindness in greater measure.

Lord, may we be attentive to your words and your works, and eager to do all that you say. In your precious name, Jesus, amen.

Day 8: Evening
PURSUE JOY

Because it spreads from you to the world

For a year and more, Amy's sister Jonelle walked a trail near her house during a daily morning prayer call.

Then Jonelle hosted a birthday party for her daughter. Mixing the various personalities together was a bit of a rough go.

She had organized a scavenger hunt game throughout the trail, and the group headed out.

She told Amy later, "We started out down a side path shortcut that I don't normally walk. And everybody was a bit off. Grumpiness and bickering.

"But as soon as we hit the trail where I walk and pray, everybody re-centered, and peace prevailed."

Do you see what this means?

When we walk the land, we create *actual pathways* in the Spirit.

Jonelle walked the land, and every person who walked that land later reaped the benefit of her prayers.

But this is biblical!

For you shall go out in joy and be led forth in peace; the mountains and the hills before you shall break forth into singing, and all the trees of the field shall clap their hands.

Instead of the thorn shall come up the cypress; instead of the brier shall come up the myrtle; and it shall make a name for the LORD, an everlasting sign that shall not be cut off.[34]

———— • ✸ • ————

Lord God, as your people go out, the land rejoices.

I'm asking, Lord, for an upgrade in our ability to believe that we actually do change the environment around us.

Lord, I'm asking for a release of your people to shift the environment away from thorns and briers, to far more productive plants. Cypress wood built ships and instruments. Oil from the myrtle plant's leaves was used for medicine.

Transform the places of pain and ugliness into beauty, productivity, and healing.

May the land rejoice as your children recognize and expect the glory that we carry to transform the world around us. In the name of Jesus, amen.

Day 9: Morning

PURSUE THE KINGDOM OF HEAVEN

Because I want to see the dead raised

Jesus told his disciples, "As you go, proclaim this: the Kingdom of Heaven has come near. Heal the sick, raise the dead, cleanse those who have leprosy, drive out demons. Freely you have received; freely give."[35]

This statement startles me.

As I look at my life, I haven't yet seen the dead raised.

But I have seen demons driven out.

I have seen the sick healed.

I'm not sure why Jesus lists leprosy in its own category ... perhaps because it stood for the most outrageous of miracles, like healing AIDS or paralysis. *Lord, increase my faith!*

But raising the dead?

If I have not because I ask not ... Workplace Prayer client Carla Pratico said, "I've not been to a funeral in the last decade without asking the Lord for resurrection. Because Jesus said that we'd do greater works than he did, and he raised the dead. So I want to see it, too."

Another client wrote, *I don't have that power, but he does. And so I ask that I could be present, or walk a path, where I would be in* that situation where God wanted to raise a dead person. It's written that's our job ... and I haven't ever seen that done.

But maybe I have. When someone comes into contact with Jesus, their sins are forgiven and those who are dead begin to live.

There are some dead people walking that I'd sure like to see come alive.

So I'm asking.

Miracles abound. Dead people live! Let's do this!

Let us pray.

———— • ❀ • ————

Lord, we ask that we would be prepared and excited to heal the sick, raise the dead, cleanse those who have leprosy, and drive out demons.

We praise you, Lord, that you tell us that we have freely received, and that we get to freely give.

We're asking that you would do it again in this generation, that you would do it again for us.

Thank you, Lord, that when the disciples returned after having had these instructions, Lord, that you said, "I saw Satan fall like lightning from heaven." Your instructions were efficacious in this world.

Send us out to be efficacious for your kingdom as well.

In the name of Jesus Christ, amen.

Day 9: Evening
PURSUE BUILDING AND RESTORATION

Because this is part of your call

I am curious: does this list apply to you?

- Do you seek to avoid oppressing others?
- Do you try not to accuse, but seek to absolve?
- Do you keep from speaking maliciously, but speak with kindness instead?
- Do you spend yourself on behalf of the needy?
- Do you satisfy the needs of the oppressed?

Because if so, Isaiah 58 says that you have an incredible string of promises coming your way.

- Your light will rise in the darkness.
- Your night will become like the noonday.
- The Lord will guide you always.
- He will satisfy your needs in a sun-scorched land.
- He will strengthen your frame.
- You will be like a well-watered garden, like a spring whose waters never fail.
- You will rebuild the ancient ruins.

- You will raise up the age-old foundations.
- You will be called Repairer of Broken Walls, Restorer of Streets with Dwellings.

I didn't sit down one day and, in a burst of creative writing, invent this list.

And it's not a collection of "wouldn't it be nice" ideas.

You don't need to exercise the power of positive thinking.

No.

These are the promises of God.

And because he is not a man that he should lie,[36] these promises are true.

———— • ❈ • ————

To any spirit of weariness, to any spirit of discouragement, to any place in us that feels so deeply how tiring it can be to have long obedience in the same direction, I speak to those spirits. I bind them and send them to you, Jesus. And in the place of them, Lord, I ask that you would bless us with the full blessings of Isaiah 58.

Lord, thank you for these amazing promises. Thank you that we get to be the light of the world. Thank you that the darkness around us does not remain darkness, and that you guide us. Thank you for your constant provision, and that you strengthen us to stand up to any amount of pressure.

Thank you for the picture of us as a well-watered garden. Thank you that we are not a vernal spring, one that dries up in warm weather, but a spring whose waters never fail.

Thank you that the places that are in ruins do not have to remain in ruins. That we get to proclaim you, Jesus, as the foundation, the perfect cornerstone.

Thank you for the names we are called: Repairer of Broken Walls, Restorer of Streets with Dwellings.

Amen. May it be so, in the name of Jesus.[37]

Day 10: Morning
PURSUE NURTURING

But do it from your overflow

On a prayer call, two people prayed really different prayers, both around the same theme.

The first person facilitates a community. Within that community, some people ask for prayer. But how to handle requests from people struggling with fear and anxiety?

The second person grieves over struggling family members, for the pain and darkness that they carry, for the ways that the body of Christ has been a source of hurt, rather than encouragement.

In both of these cases, the central question could be described as, "How do I nurture and nourish the people around me?"

Here's my favorite passage on this topic.

When they had finished eating, Jesus said to Simon Peter, "Simon son of John, do you love me more than these?"

"Yes, Lord," he said, "you know that I love you."

Jesus said, "Feed my lambs."

Again Jesus said, "Simon son of John, do you love me?"

He answered, "Yes, Lord, you know that I love you."

Jesus said, "Take care of my sheep."

The third time he said to him, "Simon son of John, do you love me?"

Peter was hurt because Jesus asked him the third time, "Do you love me?" He said, "Lord, you know all things; you know that I love you."

Jesus said, "Feed my sheep.[38]

Jesus told Peter what to do, presumably with the expectation that *this would be possible*.

The Lord always supplied Peter's needs. He will do the same for you.

We aren't sent out empty. We're sent out with the power of God.

———— · ✹ · ————

Lord, I'm asking that you would fill us with all that you have for us to be able to bless this broken and hurting world.

Lord, I'm asking for your rivers of living water to flow in us and through us and go out to a parched world.

Lord, you are the only one who satisfies. And I ask, Lord, that we would continually be in your feast, and in your stream, Lord, that we would not be seeking to replenish others out of something that is not already given to us, but that we would replenish others from your overflow.

Thank you, Jesus.

Day 10: Evening
PURSUE EMOTIONAL HEALTH

Because this, too, is part of your benefits package

One month, Amy heard multiple stories of healing from anxiety or mental anguish.

Even if you don't struggle with anxiety, celebrate the goodness of God found in these testimonies.

First story: a friend of Amy's was a tenured college professor who loved to teach. He taught in college classrooms. He taught high school Sunday school.

But when asked to preach, he would have *tremendous* anxiety. His wife said, "Think of 20 hours of anxiety for a 20 minute talk. It was so bad that it got to the point where I wasn't sure it was worth it."

After laboring under this for some years, finally he said, "Lord, I am giving you one more year to get through this. And if this isn't changed in a year, I'll be done."

He was scheduled to preach eight times that coming year, about once a month during the school year, for services related on healing prayer.

The first one or two months were still agony. The next few months had their moments of tension.

But by about month six, the anxiety was gone, and has stayed gone.

Thanks be to God.

Second story comes from Koryn R. She wrote:

I have struggled with low-level anxiety the majority of my life without understanding it or realizing how much it was affecting my life.

The Lord had already been showing me the importance of emotional health and inviting him in to heal these areas.

I was studying and reading my Bible at a local coffee shop, and for some reason I ended up in Ecclesiastes 9.

When I read Ecclesiastes 9:7, my view of God forever changed.

It says, "Go eat your bread with joy and drink your wine with a merry heart, for I have already approved what you do."

Something happened in that moment.

It was only a week later when he revealed to me that the root issue of my anxiety was control. He freed me from anxiety in an instant in December 2018, and I have not had anxiety ever since.

I have a sense of Peace and Freedom that I've never felt before, and it has been life changing.

I now know without a doubt that Jesus loves me unconditionally, and he even likes me and delights in me!

Thanks be to God!

Third story comes from Jodi R. She wrote:

I went through breast cancer about 10 years ago, when our twins were 9 months old. Up to that point I had never relied on the prayers of others. I was very private and didn't enjoy sharing my struggles. Through that difficult time I learned how much I needed the prayers of others. I was astonished by the power of praying brothers and sisters.

I learned to ask for prayer, and to be specific. Of course I longed for total healing, but I also struggled with anxiety as night fell. I requested prayer specifically for when the sun was setting, that I would experience the LORD's peace.

People prayed, and I was delivered from that anxiety ... even before I knew what the outcome of diagnosis would be.

Thanks be to God!

Fourth story comes from pastor Bill Johnson, as part of a conference keynote.

I remember as a pastor being so discouraged. Finally I'd go down to the church late at night, and of course I'd be there all by myself. And I'd walk through that sanctuary, and I could pray for hours and have nothing happen.

It's embarrassing.

But I shouldn't say nothing happened, it just it didn't change me. You know, I'm sure God was blessing everybody I was praying for, but I was still a mess.

And finally, I remember one evening when I was down there late at night, it hit me: "Maybe I should rejoice."

That's the last thing I feel like doing.

I'm depressed, I'm discouraged, I've got this cloud over me that I invited. In fact, I've empowered this thing. My thought life has made this thing very happy.

And I thought, "I should rejoice."

So I did. I begin to dance. I began to shout. I began to do all the stuff that was a complete violation of how I felt inside.

And it's the craziest thing—those clouds just left so fast.

Oppression can't stand the presence of joy.

We have this misunderstanding about joy. Most people think that joy is what enables them to rejoice. That's in the world.

In the kingdom, rejoicing creates joy. The joy of the Lord is our strength. We're only as strong as our joy.

I don't need an external experience to find joy.

I just have to make the right choices and celebrate his goodness even when I'm under that cloud.

He concluded that part of his talk by saying, "The key to emotional health is rejoicing always."

Thanks be to God!

Did you notice that all four of these testimonies are all completely different?

- One combined diligent action with a prayer of desperation for healing over some months.
- One took truth from the Word of God and a moment of revelation to cut off anxiety in an instant.
- One involved the wider church community to offer up prayers.
- One used action completely opposite to the natural inclination, but in obedience to the call of God.

Several of my mentors talk about testimonies. "If you hear a testimony, you can claim it for your own life, too."

Or, a variation of this idea, says, "The thing that Jesus heals in you can become your place of greatest ministry."

If you are struggling under the weight of anxiety, God is with you. May he give you full healing and blessing and peace. What he has done for others he can do for you.

———— • ✸ • ————

Lord God, you say in your word that you not given us the spirit of fear; but of power, and of love, and of a sound mind. The spirit of fear is not part of your plan for us. Thank you, God! Thank you for the testimonies of the saints, that you work in each of us specifically and uniquely. I ask, Lord, that you would do for all who struggle what you have done already—heal and restore. Any spirit of anxiety, of depression, of worry, of discord, we see you and refuse to partner with you. Be gone. And in the place of that darkness, we ask, Jesus, that you would pour out the oil of gladness, rejoicing, trust, peace, rest, joy. Lord, give your children the life abundantly that you promise. Pour it out, Lord!

We give you thanks for your goodness and your healing power. Amen and amen!

Day 11: Morning
PURSUE EASTER EGGS

Because God is a God of delightful surprises

Rabbi Lapin taught about the number 92.

First he pointed out that there are 92 naturally occurring elements from Hydrogen to Uranium.[39]

Then he explained that the creation account in the Hebrew scripture stretches from Genesis 1:1 through 2:3, and it uses 92 distinct words. Some phrases repeat ("there was evening and there was morning"), but if you don't count words more than once, in Hebrew, that passage uses 92 unique words.

And then he brought in Psalm 92. "For you make me glad by your deeds, Lord; I sing for joy at what your hands have done. How great are your works, Lord, how profound your thoughts!"[40]

Ninety-two elements. Ninety-two words. Psalm 92, a psalm of creation.

But here's the shocking thing: the 92nd element wasn't discovered until 1939. The earliest outline of the Periodic Table of the Elements was just 70 years before that, when Mendeleev first outlined an early version in 1869.

But all along, a little Easter egg hidden in the Bible. Hidden, but in plain sight when the time was right.

I want a greater ability to recognize these Easter eggs.

I want open eyes to see all the myriad ways that God is at work, and to celebrate what he's done.

——————— • ✱ • ———————

Lord, I join with the psalmist to say, "You make me glad by your deeds, Lord! I sing for joy at what your hands have done! How great are your works, Lord! How profound your thoughts!"

You astonish me with your details and your sense of fun and your continuous graciousness.

You put gifts in your word, you put gifts in your creation, you put gifts in our life stories.

Thank you that it is your glory to conceal a matter, and our glory to seek it out. Thank you for the Easter eggs around us, for us to go and uncover and cherish and treasure.

Lord, give us eyes to see. May we be sensitive to the move of your Spirit in our lives.

Thank you, Lord, that you are that good.

And as verse eight says, "You, Lord, are forever exalted."

Amen. And Amen.

Day 11: Evening
PURSUE THE CALL OF GOD

Even if you don't have all the support you might wish

Once Amy left a meeting not feeling heard. Grumpy and irritated, when she went to bed, she had a feeling of being a bit more exposed, a bit less protected, than she preferred.

The Lord woke her up in the night, and she pulled out *Let's Just Laugh at That* by Steve Backlund.[41]

Each page begins with a different lie that we're supposed to laugh at. In this case: "I Cannot Fulfill My Call Because of the People in My Life."

Oh. Hmm.

That's a lie?

It felt true right up until she read that it was a lie.

Next: the laughable assumptions behind this lie, including:

- *God is surprised and completely hindered by what the people in my life are doing. Their choices make it impossible for my calling to be fulfilled.*
- *The fulfillment of my calling is more determined by others than by me.*
- *What is happening in my life cannot possibly be used of God to give me even greater influence and ministry.*

- *If a relationship isn't instantly beneficial, it can't take me to my calling.*[42]

After the lie comes the truth.

"Many godly ones have overcome difficult people."

For example: David. His dad didn't see him as the most likely candidate to be king. His brothers were not supportive. His king and boss tried to kill him. And yet he fulfilled the call of God on his life.

For example: Joseph. Almost murdered by his brothers. Enslaved. False charge of attempted rape. Languishing in prison.

Yet God's purposes went forward.

For example: Noah. If he and his family were the only righteous ones on the face of the earth, every person who surrounded them did not help move the plan of God forward.

Yet Noah fulfilled the task God gave him.

Next Steve gives strategies for overcoming this lie.

1. *Renew your beliefs about the people in your life—Begin to believe that problematic people or relationships are actually opportunities to go higher in God.*

2. *Believe in the power of his calling on your life—God has an uncanny ability to cause us to fulfill our calling despite difficult people in our lives.*

Amen. I receive that. I love that.

The page ends with three declarations.

To me, declarations are not just "power of positive thinking" ideas. Rather, I think of them like when a parent tells a child something and says, "What did I just say?" We repeat truth back to God, as a way to demonstrate that we're hearing his truth.

1. *I see people in my life as strategic opportunities, not obstacles.*

2. *I have renewed mindsets about my calling and the people in my life.*

3. Daily, I am making progress and stepping into my calling.

Amen! What a gift that God forgives us, and gives us the opportunity to repent turn a situation around.

Day 12: Morning
THE LORD'S UNEXPECTED DISCIPLINE PURSUES US

Happily so

Our fathers disciplined us for a short time as they thought best, but God disciplines us for our good, so that we may share in His holiness.[43]

The author of Hebrews acknowledges that parents act "as seemed best to them."[44] We do the best we can, but it's all a bit of a mystery.

How much better than earthly parents is God as our parent.

Paul Van Hoesen was looking at the contrast between earthly parents' discipline, and God's discipline. "God disciplines us for our *good*."

The word "good," the Greek word *sumphero*, means:

1. to bear or bring together
2. to bear together or at the same time

    a. to carry with others
    b. to collect or contribute in order to help
    c. to help, be profitable, be expedient[45]

Another reference work adds the shade of meaning: "to bring advantage."[46]

So look at this.

- God disciplines us to bring us together, making us whole (bringing us together in ourselves).
- God disciplines us to bear at the same time.
- God disciplines us to carry with others, fixing our relationships.
- God disciplines us to collect or contribute in order to help. He takes some things and gives some things in order to shape us in his image.
- God disciplines us to help.
- God disciplines us to make us profitable.
- God disciplines us so we can be expedient (convenient and practical, suitable and appropriate).
- God disciplines us to bring advantage.

With the ultimate goal, as Hebrews says, that we may share in his holiness.

With, as Hebrews says, the ultimate goal that we may share in his holiness.

Paul Van Hoesen wrote,

I am now starting to correlate failures and blessing!

It seems like the places where I really screw up, repent, feel inadequate about my ability to walk with God in that area, there comes greater blessing in that place than in the times where I think I'm self-righteously owed some blessing and then I'm a bit grumpy at God because it didn't happen yet.

"Where's my kid goat dinner God? You owe me!" —The Older Brother (paraphrased).

YIKES!

May we move forward into this next season, with the understanding that we are being disciplined by his goodness, and with expectation of wonderful things to come.

———— • ✹ • ————

Lord God, thank you that you invite us to share in your holiness. As you discipline us for our good, for our advantage, to help us and to cause us to bear, we thank you for your precision and your perfection. We welcome your voice in our lives.

In the beautiful name of Jesus, amen.

Day 12: Evening
PURSUE THE GODHEAD

Because we can pray to Father, Son, and Holy Spirit

A reader once asked, "Does God relate to us as a Mother, as well as a Father? If so, how? Is it ever appropriate to address God as our Mother?"

What a great question!

First of all, clearly the scripture does not *directly* refer to God as a mother. The scriptures contain no "goddess" language.

But that's not the whole story. Psalm 91:4 says, "He will cover you with his feathers, and under his wings you will find refuge; his faithfulness will be your shield and rampart."

Amy once had a chicken brood and hatch chicks. The rooster never once tried to nurture those babies. That was the hen's job.

And in Genesis 2:18, God notes that it's not good for Adam to be alone: "I will make him an help meet for him." The word "help" is *ezer* in Hebrew, used 21 times in the scripture. Twice it describes Eve. Three times it describes other people.

And sixteen times it refers to God as our helper.

So Eve helped Adam, far beyond making the bed and washing dishes.

Eve, presumably, helped in power.

After all, that's how God helps: in *power*.

Then there's the name *El Shaddai*, usually translated "Almighty."

But the root word *shad* is the word "breast," which means that this word might be translated "the breasted one," in the sense of nurture, provision, care, mothering.

So does God exhibit maternal aspects?

Yes.

Dawna De Silva teaches on healing prayer. In her book *Sozo*, based on the Greek word that means "saved, healed, and delivered," she points out that oftentimes people tend to address either Father God, or Jesus, or (most rarely) the Holy Spirit in their prayers.

But they don't usually address all three.

In our minds, we often equate God the Father with our earthly father. That makes sense.

What about our mother? Well, mothers are usually nurturing, teaching, and comforting. What part of the Godhead does this?

The Holy Spirit, the Comforter and teacher.[47]

Where does Jesus fit? He's our brother, and he calls us friend. He was the one who came in human form.

Sozo prayer ministers have found that if you had a challenging relationship with your father, you're going to find it hard to pray to the Father.

If you had a rocky relationship with your mother, you'll probably not want to pray to the Holy Spirit.

And if you had difficulties with siblings or friends, you might avoid praying to Jesus.

So part of a healing ministry is to help you be comfortable interacting with all three parts of the Godhead.

Healing prayer may be as simple as saying, "I don't want to pray to you, Jesus. What's the lie that I'm believing? What truth do you have for me in exchange?"

And then listen and receive what he has in exchange.

Often, as part of this process, you will find that you need to forgive.

Let me pray a blessing over us.

———— ·✸· ————

Father God, I thank you that you call us your children.

Jesus, I thank you that you came to earth and showed us what it is to live as a man.

Holy Spirit, I thank you that you are still present as our comforter and as our teacher.

I ask, that you, Father, Son, and Holy Spirit, would be present in us and at work in us this week, and all the days of our lives.

We thank you and we love you. In Jesus' name, amen.

Day 13: Morning
PURSUE THE EXTRAORDINARY SPIRIT

Because the world is full of riddles and problems

I once spoke with a client who had been cut to the heart by Daniel 5:12. Daniel "was found to have a keen mind and knowledge and understanding, and also the ability to interpret dreams, explain riddles and solve difficult problems." This verse fired my imagination. I ask God for this gift.

———— · ✳ · ————

Lord, three words came to the fore from that verse: illumination, insight, and wisdom.

Oh, Lord, may you give us illumination, revelation, wisdom, insight, foresight.

May we understand that the goal is not that we work harder. We don't need to be typical, anxious and pushing and striving. May we walk in the opposite spirit.

I think of how the Amplified Version says, "It was because an extraordinary spirit, knowledge and insight, the ability to interpret dreams, clarify riddles, and solve complex problems were found in this Daniel, whom the king named Belteshazzar. Now let Daniel be called and he will give the interpretation."

I'm asking, oh Lord, that you deposit and establish and impart this extraordinary spirit, Lord, this knowledge and intelligence. We need the ability to interpret, the power of revelation to explain, the grace to solve problems.

So I'm praying, Lord, this Daniel 5:12, in our lives, and in the communities we serve.

Lord, my son David goes into different organizations, and he said that it's amazing, that all organizations or ministries really reproduce themselves: their gifts, their talents, their styles, even their dress.

So, Lord, I'm asking that our communities would reproduce this excellent spirit of Daniel.

Lord, I also think of the favor that comes from being around people who are gifted and talented, who have a certain grace. Lord, as I think of all the different teachings, instructions, impartation, and mentoring that have taken place in our lives—Lord, we commit it all to you. We commit the journey that we have been on.

And we ask, Oh, God, would you bring an upgrade for us?

Lord, even our family lines, the strengths and weaknesses and legacy of our families, Lord, we present it to you as a fragrant aroma, as a thank offering.

We ask that the hand of God will be upon us, that the precise presence of God will be upon us.

Lord, like Daniel, may an excellent spirit be upon us, a spirit of Daniel. Not of striving, not of pushing.

But like Daniel, may the spirit of favor be upon us to open doors.

Lord, we trust you for what you're doing. May we steward the grace, the gifts, and the seasons.

May we walk in a spirit of revelation.

May we have the gift of foresight and discernment, to see and feel and interpret. May we have the grace to solve problems.

We come with a grateful heart, but we also ask for more. We want more of your kingdom. We want more of your influence. We want more of your nature to burst through us, to radiate through us.

In Jesus' name. Thank you, Lord. Amen.

Day 13: Evening
PURSUE ADVENTURE

Because life in the kingdom need not be boring

Amy describes her mentor Lisa van den Berg as one of the most pastoral people she has ever met. Lisa lives and breathes shepherding, caring for the heart of the one in front of her, seeking to deeply bless everyone she comes in contact with.

She likes to go on adventures with Jesus, as this on July 19, 2019.

———— • ✹ • ————

JESUS: Lisa, will you come on an adventure with Me?

LISA: Yes, Lord.

JESUS: Let's go and check the mail because I have something good for you.

LISA: Yay! OK, Lord!

I check the mailbox and it's empty.

LISA: Lord, it's empty. Why do You do that? I hear a prompting from You, I follow it in faith and then there's nothing there. I'm already tired from a long walk and now I'm running late to get ready for work. It seems like a waste of time, and my hopes raise, only to be dashed. Please help me understand.

JESUS: There are two lies you believe that I want to set you free from ... and an invitation to more.

Lie 1: Every moment of my time has to be productive otherwise I'm not stewarding my life well and I'll be a disappointment to God.

Lie 2: When I hear Jesus speak to me and I do what He asks, the outcome will be successful.

LISA: Yes, You're right, I do believe those things. What is the Truth You see instead?

JESUS:

Truth 1: I love you no matter what you "do" or "accomplish." Period. Simply spend your everyday life with Me.

Truth 2: Your definition of success is very different to Mine. Our trip to check the mail was successful in My eyes because I'm teaching you how to hear Me and do the things I ask, even when you don't understand.

Invitation to more: I'm developing your faith in Me regardless of whether the outcome looks successful to you or not. A time is coming when you'll need it and I want to help you develop it now.[48]

LISA: Wow, thank You for the way You love me. Thank You for breaking off the lies I believe and replacing them with Truth. I'll go and check an empty mailbox with You anytime.

JESUS: Me too. I love spending your life with you.[49]

———— • ✱ • ————

Lord Jesus, how beautiful.

May we, too, be released to have such adventures with you.

Lord Jesus, thank you for this precious example of how you gently guide and teach us, even when we feel a bit grumpy or confused or frustrated. Thank you for your patience and kindness, and that you free us from lies to walk in your truth.

I ask, Lord, that what you do for Lisa, you do also for us. Open our ears so that we can hear your voice, inviting us to adventures with you. May we be eager to exchange our lies for your truth. Speak to us clearly, and may we be ever more able to hear your voice. May we come to recognize more clearly the spontaneous thoughts that cross our mind, those which are so much more gentle, gracious, and kind than our own. Thank you for being in our lives. May we walk ever more closely with you. Thank you that you are able to do more than all we ask or imagine. In your holy and precious name, amen.

Day 14: Morning
PURSUE SURRENDER

Because God owns it all anyway

On the *Real Faith Stories* podcast with Brian Robinson, several people talked about how they turned their business over to God.

Some did this as a prayer. Some did it as a ceremony, complete with deed and witnesses.

In each case, the business owners acknowledged that God gives us things, and then we give them back to him.

For some time now, this scripture has been ringing in my head:

At each and every sunrise you will hear my voice
as I prepare my sacrifice of prayer to you.
Every morning I lay out the pieces of my life on the altar
and wait for your fire to fall upon my heart.[50]

What an evocative image!

We pray for ourselves, and we pray for our clients, over and over: *Lord, I put the pieces of my life on your altar, and wait for your fire to fall.*

He gives us life, and then we give our life back to him.

———— · ✸ · ————

Lord, thank you for life and work and all that you've called us to do and put in our hands.

We give you our lives and our work and our calling, and we put it in your hands.

We are yours, Lord.

Day 14: Evening
PURSUE REST

Jesus promises this

Jesus is always so beautiful.

After speaking for some time to a crowd in Galilee, he ended with this familiar passage:

"Come to me, all you who are weary and burdened, and I will give you rest. Take my yoke upon you and learn from me, for I am gentle and humble in heart, and you will find rest for your souls. For my yoke is easy and my burden is light."[51]

Directly after this promise, the disciples picked grain and ate it on the Sabbath. Jesus declared himself Lord of the Sabbath, and said that it is lawful to do good on the Sabbath.

Then he healed on the Sabbath, which was so horrifying to the Jews that they began, from that time, to plot how they might kill him.

Weary and burdened?

Jesus gives rest.

Not according to rigid rules.

Not by following the letter of the law in a way that restricts goodness and healing.

No. The rest that he gives is *himself.*

————— • ✸ • —————

*Lord Jesus, thank you that you taught, and continue to teach,
how to live.*

*Thank you for the gift that Eugene Peterson offered in his
translation* The Message.

*"Are you tired? Worn out? Burned out on religion? Come to me.
Get away with me and you'll recover your life. I'll show you how to
take a real rest. Walk with me and work with me—watch how I do
it. Learn the unforced rhythms of grace. I won't lay anything heavy
or ill-fitting on you. Keep company with me and you'll learn to live
freely and lightly."*

*Thank you that we get to walk with you and work with
you. Amen.*

Day 15: Morning
GOD PURSUES SONSHIP FOR YOU

He has compassion for you, even in the place of shame

So he got up and went to his father. But while he was still a long way off, his father saw him and was filled with compassion for him; he ran to his son, threw his arms around him and kissed him.[52]

Revisit this snippet from the story of the prodigal son. When you've made a mistake, messed up, sinned—has this been the response to you?

- His father saw him coming. Filled with love and compassion, he ran to his son, embraced him, and kissed him.[53]
- He felt compassion for his son and ran out to him, enfolded him in an embrace, and kissed him.[54]
- The father raced out to meet him, swept him up in his arms, hugged him dearly, and kissed him over and over with tender love.[55]

At your point of greatest shame, do you feel embraced with your Father's love?

Not only in your personal life, but also in any ministry,

in any business: have you given, or received, the heart of the Father?

Most people, most leaders, most businesses, and most organizations that I've seen, run on the policy: hire, fire, perform, perform. So in this passage of scripture, when the father embraced the son, kissed him, loved him, and pulled him deep into his heart, this demonstrates something about sonship. It's not based on your performance, not based on having perfect grades, not about being the best soloist in the school cantata, not being the star or the captain of an athletic team.

———— ·✦· ————

Lord, reveal to us the Father's love, the approval that God gives, and what it is to be a son.

Do a deep work in us. Let us know and experience how the Father gave his love, and how the son had to receive the Father's love.

May we be channels of the Father's love to the world around us. As we receive freely from our heavenly Father, teach us to act and think with the mind of Christ.

Give us all the healing we need, Lord, so we no longer feel shame or guilt.

Teach us the tender balance, Lord, of humility and authority as sons, with gratitude for who we are, because of who you've made us to be.

In Jesus' name, we thank you for the grace of God on our lives. Thank you that you're showing us that all things work together for good for those who love you and follow your plans. Amen.

Day 15: Evening

PURSUE AN INCREASE AND OVERFLOW OF LOVE

Or, rather, let God do this for you

As Amy and I prayed for the messages this third week, I felt strongly that we should feature the apostolic prayers as a blessing for you.

At first, Amy felt like this was cheating. Don't we need to share new content?

But I wonder if part of the call for the last four months is for us to ask, "What has the Lord already put in our hands, that we can deploy effectively without striving?"

Our prayer for you is that these words will be made new to you, that you will receive them in a new way, with a new depth of insight.

May you enjoy an apostolic blessing every evening.

———— • ❋ • ————

May the Lord make your
Love
Increase and
Overflow

For each other and
For everyone else,
Just as ours does for you.

May he
Strengthen your hearts
So that you will be

Blameless and
Holy

In the presence of our God and Father
When our Lord Jesus comes
With all his holy ones.[56]

Day 16: Morning
PURSUE MANY GOOD DAYS

Instructions included!

Come my children, listen to me, I will teach you the fear of the Lord. Whoever of you loves life and desires to see many good days, keep your tongue from evil and your lips from telling lies. Turn from evil and do good; seek peace and pursue it.[57]

In this beautiful passage, David teaches his children the fear of the Lord, seeking generational faithfulness.

The fear of the Lord "means much more than the English concept of fear. It also implies submission, awe, worship, and reverence."[58]

How beautiful, to have a parent teach awe and obedience, wonder and worship, astonishment and reverence.

Not terror, but wonder at the glory of the Lord.

David taught those who love life and desire to see many good days.

I know that I have not always loved life. I've had entire years that felt like a weighty slog.

Did I desire to see many good days? I'm sure "good days" sounded good, but I was skeptical that I could see them.

Healing prayer minister Judith MacNutt said that more

than 90% of the people who come to her ministry deal with some form of self-loathing. Usually part of healing prayer is encouraging people to want to see many good days.

May we have an upgrade in hope and eager expectation.

I would have expected a longer list on how to love life and see many good days, and I'm not sure I would have chosen these six basic instructions.

The guiding principles, here, for a good life:

1. Keep your tongue from evil. Stop with accusations and unkindness. Stay silent if you must, or speak encouragement, identity, edification, blessing.

2. Keep your lips from telling lies. Jesus says of the devil: "He was a murderer from the beginning, not holding to the truth, for there is no truth in him. When he lies, he speaks his native language, for he is a liar and the father of lies." [59] Don't side with him. Tell the truth.

3. Turn from evil. If you're going in the wrong direction, the first thing to do is stop going that direction.

4. Do good. Do what's right. Be an imitator of Christ

5. Seek peace. Other translations say, "search for peace" or "strive for peace." Don't look for ways to be at odds.

6. Pursue peace. Or "work to maintain it" or "promote it." Once you have peace, hang on to it. Nurture it. Cultivate it. Celebrate it.

Philippians 4:7 says, "And the peace of God, which transcends all understanding, will guard your hearts and your minds in Christ Jesus." We receive peace that passes understanding.

———— •✿• ————

Lord, may we walk always toward the peace that passes understanding. And if something is not tending toward peace, then please make that obvious, and give us the needed course correction.

May these instructions be fruitful in our lives, Lord, as we look forward to seeing many good days. In the name of Jesus, amen.

Day 16: Evening
PURSUE WHAT'S IN YOUR HAND

And the fruitfulness therein

For this reason, since the day we heard about you,
We have not stopped praying for you.

We continually ask God to fill you
With the knowledge of his will
Through all the
Wisdom and
Understanding
That the Spirit gives, so that you may

Live a life

Worthy of the Lord and
Please him in every way:
Bearing fruit in every good work,
Growing in the knowledge of God, being

Strengthened with all power
According to his glorious might

So that you may have
Great endurance and
Patience, and

Giving joyful thanks to the
Father, who has
Qualified you to
Share in the
Inheritance of his
Holy people in the kingdom of light.

For he has

Rescued us from
The dominion of darkness and
Brought us into
The kingdom of the Son he loves,

In whom we have redemption, the forgiveness of sins.[60]

Day 17: Morning

PURSUE BOTH THE WORK AND THE GRACE

Because breakthrough is coming

Perry Marshall's book *Memos from the Head Office* is one of my favorite resources for learning to hear God's voice better. He offers instruction and a collection of stories.

In one of my favorite insights, he writes:

I have never found the Head Office to be a substitute for:

- *Discipline*
- *Research*
- *Finding and cultivating friendships*
- *Accurate numbers and figures*
- *Testing and experimentation*
- *Healthy habits and lifestyles*
- *Developing your talents and skills*

Each of us has to do the work, and then, sometimes, we get a boost.

Amy was thinking about this need to do the work when she was homeschooling her boys. They had been reading through the history of science.

In 1869, scientists had isolated 63 elements, but they had no arrangement. They were simply a messy pile of data.

Joy Hakim, in *Newton at the Center*, describes Mendeleyev's process. "He lists the elements by their atomic weight and he also lists them by other characteristics: specific gravity, specific heat, density, state of the element at room temperature (solid, liquid, gas), valence (ability to combine with other atoms), and so on....

"He puts a few elements with similar properties on a horizontal line, including their atomic weights. Those weights vary widely. He sees no sense in them. On a second line, under the first, he sits a different group of elements and their atomic weights. Under that he puts a third group. Then his eye takes him vertically, straight down instead of across. Looked at this way, the weights, for no reason he can imagine, do seem to follow a pattern."

Then he creates playing cards of sorts for each element, rearranging. But still ... no breakthrough.

"Exhausted, he puts his bushy head on his hands and falls asleep at the desk. Then, in his words, 'I saw in a dream a table where all the elements fell into place as required. Awakening, I immediately wrote it down on a piece of paper.'"

What he wrote, then, was a very early version of the Periodic Table.

Even that was not perfect, as the Periodic Table has needed significant revision over time.

Mendeleyev had put in the work, and then his brain was ready the flash of inspiration, the heavenly boost.

Which is all to say: if, at times, the tasks you're called to do take more time and effort than you wish: do the work, but ask for the boost, too.

———— • ✻ • ————

Lord Jesus, your word tells us that "we have the mind of Christ." [61] *Thank you that we get to work in partnership with you. Yes, we do the work, but we also can ask you to support and sustain us. Thank you, Jesus. Amen.*

Day 17: Evening
PURSUE FRUITION

So lovely a word

A gardener once emphasized how astonishing fruit is: take macronutrients like potassium and magnesium (described as metallic, bitter, salty), calcium (think chalk), phosphorus (smells like garlic), as well as things like sulfur (rotten eggs), and iron (rusty nails). Combine with sunshine and water to produce a peach.

What?!

When we are told to be "fruitful," this seems at least as miraculous.

God takes all the pieces of our lives, that seem to be so random and disparate, some painful or embarrassing or unproductive ... and somehow, miraculously, creates fruitfulness.

———————— • ❈ • ————————

With this in mind,
We constantly pray for you,
That our God may make you worthy of his calling,
And that by his power
He may bring to

Fruition

Your every desire for goodness
And your every deed prompted by faith.

We pray this so that
The name of our Lord Jesus
May be glorified in you,
And you in him,
According to the grace of our God
And the Lord Jesus Christ.[62]

Day 18: Morning

PURSUE PRAYER FOR THE SHIFT

Because prayer works

We live in a world with powerful forces, powerful individuals, powerful governments, powerful corporations.

At times we feel abandoned, alone, isolated, helpless and hopeless.

In the midst of this depressing list of feelings, one day I prayed, "Lord, we lean into you, Jesus. We trust you, Lord. Thank you."

And while I prayed, Amy thought, *Oh, goodness. All those powerful individuals. They have the money; they control the narrative. What on earth can we do except pray?*

And this wasn't a hopeful thought for her, but a resigned, hopeless thought.

For a second.

But then it was like her backbone strengthened, and she remembered: *Oh! But we can PRAY!*

As Amy and I have been praying for businesses, we have witnessed again and again that our prayers *actually* make a difference.

We see solopreneurs find breakthrough for funding, and

large scale corporations shift from a destructive path to a more healthy one.

It gives our faith a boost to be able to say, "If we pray about something, God hears our prayers."

———— • ✺ • ————

So, Lord, move in power. We acknowledge that you are actually stronger than all the powerful individuals in this earth. Your resources are more infinite; your love for your people far stronger.

We invite you, Lord, into our lives and into our communities. God of hope, be present in every situation. Thank you, Lord. Amen.

Day 18: Evening
PURSUE INCOMPARABLY GREAT POWER

Specifically for us who believe

Amy and I once led a prayer call where we asked people to bring verses about power.

It was surprisingly rough going.

As we debriefed later, we realized: though the church might talk about God's glory, we talk less about his power.

And we certainly don't think about how to ask him to use his power on our behalf.

That's a pity.

Paul prayed that the church at Ephesus would know God's incomparably great power for us who believe—the same power that raised Christ from the dead and seated him above all other powers.

Enter in to this amazing reality.

———— • ❋ • ————

I keep asking that the God of our Lord Jesus Christ,
The glorious Father,
May give you
The Spirit of wisdom and revelation,

So that you may know him better.

I pray that the eyes of your heart may be enlightened
In order that you may know

The hope to which he has called you,
The riches of his glorious inheritance in his holy people,
And his incomparably great power for us who believe.

That power is the same as the mighty strength
He exerted when he raised Christ from the dead
And seated him at his right hand in the heavenly realms

Far above all rule and authority,
Power and dominion,
And every name that is invoked,
Not only in the present age
But also in the one to come.

And God placed all things under his feet
And appointed him to be head over everything

For the church,
Which is his body,
The fullness of him
Who fills everything
In every way.[63]

Day 19: Morning
PURSUE MEDITATION, DAY AND NIGHT

Focus on the good

Blessed is the one who does not walk in step with the wicked or stand in the way that sinners take or sit in the company of mockers, but whose delight is in the law of the LORD, and who meditates on his law day and night.[64]

The Hebrew word *meditate* does not mean *empty your mind.* Rather, it means *murmur, ponder, imagine, meditate, mourn, mutter, roar, speak, study, talk, utter.*

The word Hebrew word *meditate* shows up 25 times in the scripture, including this use: *This is what the LORD says to me: "As a lion growls, a great lion over its prey—and though a whole band of shepherds is called together against it, it is not frightened by their shouts or disturbed by their clamor—so the LORD Almighty will come down to do battle on Mount Zion and on its heights."*[65]

The word *growls* is the same word *meditate.*

If you've seen a house cat with a mouse, you know that even nice cats growl if you come near their prey: "This is mine to enjoy ... keep away."

How does this apply to meditating on the scripture?

Take this wonderful verse as an example: "Taste and see that the Lord is good; blessed is the one who takes refuge in him."[66]

First, we consider whether we actually believed this is true. Intellectually, sure, we could assent. "Yes, of course, God is good."

But, really, in my day-to-day life, do we doubt?

My life has, at times, seemed like an absolute disaster.

The call, then, is to align my thoughts with God's thoughts.

The Lord is good. Blessed are those who take refuge in him.

The truth is that God created me and sustains me.

The truth is that he is ever creative in his ability to heal and restore.

The truth is that he loves me as a father loves his children.

The truth is that he mourns over the hurt places of my life and celebrates even the smallest success.

The truth is that Jesus is the great physician and the one who ever lives to make intercession—to stand in the gap—for me.

The truth is that the Holy Spirit comes as a comforting presence, as a counselor to guide me, and to act as legal counsel to protect me from the accuser.

The truth is that I do have an enemy, but I have weapons and tools to defeat the enemy.

Basically: I have to preach to myself that the scripture is true, and in any way that my thoughts don't align with God's thoughts, I need to come into alignment with what he says.

—————— • ❀ • ——————

Lord, you say to "taste and see." Wow. You actually give me samples of yourself. You don't require me to follow you sight unseen, but, like an ice cream shop, you invite me to taste whether I actually like you or not. Thank you.

Lord, I love how gracious you are, that you show yourself to me. I love that you have no concern that when I taste, I might think you are bad. No. Taste and see that the Lord is good. Thank you for that truth.

And, Lord, you say, "Blessed is the one who takes refuge in you." This is not just true for other people. This is true for me.

Show me, Lord, what it looks like to taste your goodness today. *Thank you. Amen.*

Day 19: Evening
PURSUE GRASPING THE LOVE OF GOD

The dimensions keep expanding

When we follow Jesus, we might expect that we simply need to grasp some basic concepts: redemption, restoration, forgiveness, sonship, grace, and so on.

But perhaps we don't get to simply check these off the mental list.

I wonder if all of these words have ever greater depths to plumb, ever greater heights to climb ... starting now and going into eternity.

Dr. Pete Carter, in his book *Unwrapping Lazarus*, tells of a talk by professor David Ford, who teaches on what he calls a "continually developing theology." He believes that we can't ever come to firm definitions of God: "Otherwise it can't be God, but only our limited thoughts about him."

Dr. Carter continues, "If God is eternal and infinite, then there is no end to His being, so there is always more to discover about Him. If theology is knowing Him [because the word itself literally means "the knowledge of God"], rather than just knowing about Him, then our theology should be ever developing."[67]

I think Paul himself has a similar desire for those he prays for, especially about the love of Christ.

Read his glorious prayer from the perspective that there is more to grasp, more richness to enter into.

———— • ❋ • ————

I pray that
Out of his glorious riches
He may strengthen you
With power
Through his Spirit
In your inner being,

So that Christ
May dwell in your hearts through faith.

And I pray that you,
Being rooted
And established
In love, may have
Power,
Together with all the Lord's holy people,
To grasp

How wide
And long
And high
And deep
Is the love of Christ,

And to know this love
That surpasses knowledge—
That you may be filled
To the measure of all the fullness of God.

Now to him who is able to do
Immeasurably more than all we ask
Or imagine, according to his
Power
That is at work within us,
To him be glory
In the church
And in Christ Jesus
Throughout all generations,
For ever and ever!
Amen.[68]

Day 20: Morning
PURSUE PRAYER

Because it will consume you from now into eternity

Some time ago, Amy and I were finishing a meeting with our friend Paul Van Hoesen. I asked him to pray, and Amy had a flicker of a thought: "You should record this."

But she didn't. As she readily admits: "I don't always recognize the flickers as God flickers."

Paul prayed a beautiful, powerful prayer. That we didn't record.

A month or two later, Amy asked Paul if he remembered this prayer at all.

Yes. He could pray along those same lines again.

So rather than beating herself up for weeks and weeks ... she could have just asked.

You have not because you ask not.

There is always a solution.

May this prayer bless you as it blessed us.

———— • ❋ • ————

First Corinthians 13 says, "Now abides faith, hope, and love, these three."

Father, scripture is always a wonder to me. I always ask Holy

Spirit, why? Why would you have faith and hope, these two things, abiding forever?

I understand why love would be eternal, but faith and hope— why? We're going to know as we're known. What do I need faith for, when I can see everything?

And I heard the Holy Spirit and the Father say, that we will be forever pulling out of God, out of the Father's heart, the invisible plans he has.

This is our way of life forever.

This isn't a temporary state: "Well, you need faith here. You need to learn how to have hope here. You need to learn how to pray and pull the invisible into the visible here only, and then when you get to heaven and are finally transformed, now you won't need that anymore."

No. This is the eternal pursuit. It's an eternal muscle. These are muscles of the spirit, and these are muscles you're going to use forever. You're exercising faculties, you're awaking faculties. It's like teaching a child, and when they start learning those math tables, they start thinking differently, they start seeing differently, they start calculating.

And I see, Lord, that you are training us for eternity here. We are learning to calculate by faith and hope. We are exercising the muscle of faith and hope through prayer. We are perceiving your heart and we are going to use that muscle forever.

In fact, this is our opportunity wedge right now.

Because the world's opportunity wedge is: your wedge starts at birth and it's really wide. You have all kinds of opportunities, and then the older you get, it shrinks and shrinks and shrinks until you finally die. And the closer to death you get, the less opportunities you have. The world looks back in regret, like "Man, I wish I'd taken advantage of those opportunities."

But we're believers, and our opportunity wedge doesn't work like that.

Our opportunity wedge starts when we're born again. And it is getting wider and wider and wider as we get older. And then at some point we die, but the opportunities continue to expand because we are eternal beings. Though our outer man is decaying, our inner man is growing in strength every single day. We don't look at the things that are seen, but the things that are unseen, because the things that are seen are temporal, but the things that are unseen are eternal.

We are looking into the unseen. We are gazing into the unseen. We see the Father's heart. We see his face, we see his hidden and wonderful plans. And he's like, "Come pull this out of me. Come on, let's do this."

It's how he is. It's his nature. It's part of him. It's not a, "I'm just going to grit my teeth to this life and I'll be so glad when we're done with this faith and hope stuff. I'll be so glad when I don't have to worry about this, and I can just see and be seen."

Yes, you're going to see and be seen, but you're going forever to be pulling the invisible out of the Father. And we will forever be birthing by faith and hope, through prayer, the eternal plans of the Father into his amazing universe.

So may we push into you, Father, for every invisible thing you have available for us, a myriad of things. We can't see them. But they're buried away in your heart.

Father, we see the amazing goodness of a father like you, who sits around and listens to the whims of our heart, the, "Oh, I wish I had a drink of water from the well in Jerusalem." And like the mighty men, you run, break through the lines, and bring it back.

And Lord, we pour out our worship before you because you are so good. Your goodness is so incredibly wide and good. You listen to the whims of our heart. You know everything before we need it. You know every word on our tongue before we speak it. Lord, we're thankful.

Day 20: Evening
PURSUE DISCERNMENT

For what is best

And this is my prayer:
That your love may abound more
And more
In knowledge
And depth of insight,

So that you may be able to
Discern
What is best
And may be pure
And blameless
For the day of Christ,

Filled with the fruit of righteousness
That comes through Jesus Christ—
To the glory and praise of God.[69]

Day 21: Morning
PURSUE MORE

Because there is more for you

In Chuck Parry's book *Free Falling*, he talks about how, when he first came to the Lord, the Lord would speak to him all the time.

He had grown up entirely without a knowledge of God, and, as a hippie, asked Jesus to be his guru.

Hearing from God made sense to him.

Then, at some point, the Lord stopped speaking.

So Chuck thought that was a bit odd, but picked up a Bible, which he had never read.

He found that he couldn't get enough of it.

At some point after that, the Lord started speaking again. "I wanted you to be able to hear from me in a different way. You hear my voice, and now you see how I speak from my word."

When she heard this story, Jaime said:

When you said: I wanted to show you that you can hear from me in a different way, my heart skipped. I've had times when a friend prayed in the spirit and prophesied things into my life, but I didn't exactly seek that. When it came, it came, and it was beautiful. But I NEVER EVEN ASKED FOR IT.

When that hope and life did come, I remember feeling somehow dirty to even consider praying: "Oh, Father, that was so life-giving in the barren place I'm slogging through—can you do that again for me?"

I didn't pray it. And secretly hoped that God didn't know.

I would tell myself, "God doesn't perform on command, Jaime!"

But I am starting to see new ways that God speaks to me.

Wow.

What a year.

Can there be more?

Interesting question.

Switching from Chuck Parry to another contemporary hero of the faith, Joan Hutter told a story about Heidi Baker. Heidi was to speak at a conference, and the speaker before her was talking about how there was no more.

And I don't know the context of the message. Perhaps the speaker meant that Jesus has paid for all our sins, and therefore we have all we need.

But when Heidi got up to speak, she simply cried out, "MORE!"

Because we have not yet come to the end of all that God has for us.

————·✱·————

Lord, we cry out for more. All that you have for us.

Day 21: Evening
PURSUE THE CALL

For the rest of the year, and the rest of your life

Rejoice always,
Pray continually,
Give thanks in all circumstances;
For this is God's will for you in Christ Jesus.

Do not quench the Spirit.
Do not treat prophecies with contempt but test them all;
Hold on to what is good,
Reject every kind of evil.

May God himself, the God of peace,
Sanctify you through and through.
May your whole spirit, soul and body be kept blameless
At the coming of our Lord Jesus Christ.

The one who calls you is faithful, and
He will do it.[70]

GAME ON!

TODAY & FOREVER
PURSUE Blessing

Thank you for spending the last three weeks in a time of more extended prayer and focus. Amy and I are excited for you during these last four months of the year.

We always want to leave a time of corporate prayer with a blessing, so here is our blessing over you.

———— • ✳ • ————

Lord, thank you for this journey together over the last 21 days, and for your presence with us. Thank you for the grace and peace of God that's been upon us. Thank you that you say that our prayers are a fragrant aroma to you, Lord, that all prayer counts, and that prayer has no expiration date.

We thank you, God, for those who have journeyed together with us to know you in a greater way.

We ask for us, and our families, to experience Christ in his resurrection, in communion with the fellowship of the Holy Spirit.

Lord, we thank you for these friends who are pressing in to know you more.

Bless them indeed.

And Lord, as you spoke to Aaron the prayer warrior, and now you speak through us: the Lord bless you and keep you. The Lord make his face shine upon you and be gracious to you. The Lord lift up your countenance and give you peace.[71]

We speak the shalom of God over your lives and over the lives of your families.

We speak life over you. We speak his ways, shown to you and your loved ones. We speak the increase of his protection, the multiplication of his provision, the power to heal, the power to deliver, the power to breakthrough: for career choices, destinies, and purposes.

And, Lord, if we had one simple prayer for these friends, it would be Paul's prayer. We pray for a spirit of wisdom and revelation, in the knowledge of you.[72] *In Jesus' name, amen.*

ONE MORE APOSTOLIC PRAYER

I always thank my God for you
Because of his grace given you in Christ Jesus.

For in him you have been enriched in every way—
With all kinds of speech
And with all knowledge—
God thus confirming our testimony about Christ among you.

Therefore you do not lack any spiritual gift
As you eagerly wait for our Lord Jesus Christ to be revealed.
He will also keep you firm to the end,
So that you will be blameless on the day of our Lord Jesus Christ.

God is faithful,
Who has called you into fellowship with his Son,
Jesus Christ our Lord.[73]

NOTES

1 Matthew 6:33
2 This book is in Bob's voice. He has carried this prayer intensive for years. Amy helped take the ideas and concepts and turn them into the finished product. This was a joint effort.
3 TPT
4 New Oxford American Dictionary
5 Psalm 34:14; quoted also in I Peter 3:11
6 Proverbs 15:9
7 I Timothy 6:11
8 II Timothy 2:22
9 If you've never really looked at Nehemiah, you might enjoy the short, easy-to-read overview of the book of Nehemiah, *The Prince Protects His City.*
10 Lord's Prayer from Matthew 6:9-13 (KJV)
11 DeVries, John. *Why Pray?* Pp. 70-74.
12 Psalm 23:6
13 https://www.blueletterbible.org/lexicon/h7291/kjv/wlc/0-1/ Found 2/1/2022.
14 John 14:16
15 Psalm 7:10 (TPT)
16 Psalm 16:8 (TPT)
17 Psalm 62:1-2 (TPT)
18 Psalm 84:9 (TPT)
19 Hebrews 12:1-2
20 I Corinthians 9:24-25
21 Matthew 6:15
22 Mark 8:17-18 NKJV
23 Notes taken by Amy in person at Bethel Redding on May 31, 2021.
24 III John 1:2
25 I Corinthians 6:19
26 Psalm 90:10
27 *God, Improv, and the Art of Living,* pp. 23-24
28 John 2:1-11
29 Psalm 8:5
30 II Corinthians 10:5
31 Genesis 1:2
32 *The Fourfold Path of Healing,* Dr. Thomas Cowan, p. 199
33 Psalm 33:22 NASB
34 Isaiah 55:12-13 (ESV)
35 Matthew 10:7-8
36 Numbers 23:19
37 Just in case you want to read those good words again, here is Isaiah 58:9b-12:
"If you do away with the yoke of oppression, with the pointing finger and malicious talk, and if you spend yourselves in behalf of the hungry and satisfy the needs of the oppressed, then your light will rise in the darkness, and your night will become like the noonday.
The Lord will guide you always; he will satisfy your needs in a sun-scorched land and will strengthen your frame.
You will be like a well-watered garden, like a spring whose waters never fail. Your people will rebuild the ancient ruins and will raise up the age-old foundations; you will be called Repairer of Broken Walls, Restorer of Streets with Dwellings."
38 John 21:15-17
39 Yes, the total number of elements today is officially far more,

but the elements after 92
are manmade.

40 Psalm 92:4-5

41 I highly recommend it: so compact
and dense and thoughtful
and helpful.

42 Italics in this evening's reading are
direct quotes from the book.

43 Hebrews 12:10 (Berean
Study Bible)

44 Hebrews 12:10 (NASB)

45 *Thayer's Greek Lexicon*

46 *Strong's Concordance*

47 John 14:26

48 Isaiah 55:8-9

49 Used with permission. To
learn more about Lisa, and
access her podcast, visit
TheWaysofWisdom.com.

50 Psalm 5:3 (TPT)

51 Matthew 11:28-30

52 Luke 15:20

53 *New Living Translation*

54 *The Voice*

55 *The Passion Translation*

56 I Thessalonians 3:12-13, reformatted for emphasis

57 Psalm 34:11-14

58 Note from Proverbs 1:7, *The
Passion Translation*

59 John 8:44

60 Colossians 1:9-14, reformatted
for emphasis

61 I Corinthians 2:16

62 II Thessalonians 1:11-12,
reformatted for emphasis

63 Ephesians 1:17-23, reformatted
for emphasis

64 Psalm 1:1-2

65 Isaiah 31:4

66 Psalm 34:8

67 *Unwrapping Lazarus*, p. 82

68 Ephesians 3:16-21, reformatted
for emphasis

69 Philippians 1:9-11, reformatted
for emphasis

70 I Thessalonians 5:16-24, reformatted for emphasis

71 Numbers 6:24-26

72 Ephesians 1:17

73 I Corinthians 1:4-9, reformatted
for emphasis

ABOUT THE AUTHORS

Bob Perry has been a passionate student of prayer for more than four decades, constantly asking, "Lord, teach me to pray." He has founded and led multiple prayer initiatives that have trained and mobilized hundreds of thousands of people in prayer partnerships.

Amy Joy Lykosh loves healing and deliverance. Her heart's cry comes from the verse, "My people are destroyed for lack of knowledge" (Hosea 4:6). The author of several highly acclaimed books, she seeks to stop the destruction as best she can through writing and speaking. You can find her podcast about prayer at amyjoy.me/podcast, and get on her daily email list at amyjoy.me/dailyprayer.

Together, they run Workplace Prayer, to cover businesses in prayer, and Prayer Mentoring, to raise up healthy intercessors to bring the kingdom of God to bear in their lives and communities.

They love feedback. Email amy@workplaceprayer.com to start a conversation.

THE PRINCE PROTECTS HIS CITY
Nehemiah Prayed Four Months, Then Rebuilt the Wall in Only 52 Days

Such a great story! But how easy to miss!

Nehemiah wasn't a warrior or a king. He was a tremendous administrator, a gifted leader, a world-class historian, a treasured friend, a successful fund-raiser, and a prince. Though he was never a CEO, he headed an enormous public works project he had planned, then served as governor for twelve years. And he prayed constantly. A free verse look at the book of Nehemiah. Come meet a man who brought God's kingdom to bear in his work.

> "I finished reading it today! Loved it. Such a nice quick pace to read Nehemiah and also space to sit in parts if I just wanted to read one page" — **Angela**

FIND OUT MORE AT
happybooks.me/nehemiah

ONE VOICE: THE STORY OF WILLIAM WILBERFORCE
Gorgeous Story of Tenacity + Courage

Biography in verse of the man who, despite all obstacles, fought to end the Slave Trade in Great Britain. Powerful story of tenacity and courage.

> "I think it's important to know Wilberforce's story, but One Voice has become one of my absolute favourite books of all time and is SO worth buying just for the beautiful writing. I was so skeptical when I first opened it and realized it was written in free verse but oh, it's so, so special. I can't make it through without sobbing." — **Emily**

ORDER EXCLUSIVELY AT
happybooks.me/wilberforce

---

21 DAYS OF A F(E)AST
A Fast That Feels More Like a Feast

Why fasting is a joy, and why you should do it. A guide for a fast that anyone can do, even if you can't restrict calories. The four types of fasting, and how to choose. Morning and evening readings for 21 days. Stories and testimonies. Drawn from four decades of experience and wisdom. Come sit in the Lord's presence.

> "Appreciating the wealth within this book!! Such a brilliant resource!" — **Nicole**

ORDER AT
happybooks.me/feast

PRAYER REFRESH
Short Prayers to Pray Through Your Day

You don't have to completely change your life, your habits, your personality, or your social media usage in order to have a good prayer life.

This book introduces a wide variety of prayers that you can pray in a minute or less, that will fit into your day, right where you are. Don't start with hours on your knees. Start with the stray half minutes here and there. Use it as a devotional for 21 days, or read straight through.

> "The Prayer Refresh was so life changing, perspective shattering, and breathed so much, much needed life into me and our home that I long to go through it again. Regularly. Like monthly." — **Amanda**

ORDER AT
happybooks.me/refresh

JUNETEENTH: AN INVITATION TO FAST
Both the Why and the How To

Join us in a one-day fast.

> "The booklet was so helpful with the historical summary of the date (which I knew nothing about), as well as specific prayers and family examples, to guide my focused petitions. The format is beautiful, and so clearly organized! Great resource!" — **Eileen**

ORDER AT
happybooks.me/juneteenth

Made in the USA
Middletown, DE
08 August 2023

36365519R00086